USBORNE HISTORY OF BR

PREHISTORIC BRITAIN

Usborne Quicklinks

The Usborne Quicklinks Website is packed with thousands of links to all the best websites on the internet. The websites include information, video clips, sounds, games and animations that support and enhance the information in Usborne internet-linked books.

To visit the recommended websites for this book, go to the Usborne Quicklinks Website at **www.usborne.com/quicklinks** and enter the keywords **Prehistoric Britain.**

USBORNE HISTORY OF BRITAIN

PREHISTORIC BRITAIN

Written by Alex Frith
with Rachel Firth, Struan Reid and Abigail Wheatley

Illustrated by Ian McNee & Giacinto Gaudenzi

Designed by Stephen Moncrieff, Tom Lalonde & Samantha Barrett

Edited by Ruth Brocklehurst & Jane Chisholm
Consultants: Dr. Ben Roberts, British Museum
Prof. Timothy Taylor, University of Bradford

Contents

What is prehistory?

The story of life in Britain goes back to a time long, long before people existed. Even after they first arrived, it was many thousands of years before they began to write about anything. Prehistory is all about what happened before written records began.

Archaeologists and other experts have uncovered many secrets of prehistoric Britain by examining traces of the things that have survived down the ages. The remains of houses, temples, tools and even long-dead bodies have all helped to build up a picture of how the first people lived, and what it was like before anyone was there at all.

Great big Britons

Millions of years before people existed, the world was home to enormous lizard-like creatures: the dinosaurs. These were some of the oldest creatures – and certainly the biggest – ever to walk on British soil.

Prehistoric lands

At the time of the dinosaurs, the British Isles didn't yet exist. There was only one continent – Pangaea – and the land that would become Britain was in the middle of it.

Britain

Pangaea

Panthalassa Ocean

Over millions of years, the land would gradually shift until the lands, islands and oceans we know today – including the British Isles – were formed.

A different world

Dinosaurs first appeared on Earth about 230 million years ago, and lorded it over all other creatures for the next 165 million years. During this time, the British Isles didn't exist as they are today. They were by turns hot, mountainous and even, for a long time, completely underwater.

All kinds of dinosaurs lived there, from lumbering giants to fierce hunters, as well as fishlike reptiles such as the *ichthyosaurus* and the long-necked *plesiosaurus*.

This is an artist's impression of two gigantic *diplodocuses* walking through the mists of Jurassic Britain.

The era of
dinosaurs
came to an end
soon after a meteorite
struck the Earth.

Catastrophic collision

One fateful day, around 65 million years ago, a
meteorite (a giant ball of rock) from space hurtled into
the Earth, and everything changed. Earthquakes shook
the land, and volcanoes erupted all over the world.
Great clouds of dust and poisonous gases filled the sky.

    The next few thousand years were a dark and
dangerous time. Trees and other plants struggled to
grow, and the sea got much colder. Without food to
eat, many animals starved to death. Eventually, all the
dinosaurs – as well as many sea creatures and other
animals – died out for good.

First Britons

In 1824, a set of fossil
bones found in Britain
was identified as
megalosaurus – the first
dinosaur to be named.

It lived about 175
million years ago.

The oldest dinosaur
remains found in
Britain belong to
thecodontosaurus.
It lived about 210
million years ago.

Animals of ancient Britain

After the dinosaurs, but long before people arrived, all sorts of animals roamed on British soil:

Dyatrima was nearly twice the height of a person.

Hyaenodon was a deadly carnivore.

Moerterium was an early kind of elephant.

An ever-changing world

Although the dinosaurs died out, many other creatures survived. These were the ancestors of animals living today. Sharks and other fish took over the sea, while birds, and later mammals, dominated on land.

Around 50 million years ago, giant birds such as *dyatrima* lived in Britain. They couldn't fly, but they could run fast and had huge claws. Their prey were mammals, such as the small, horse-like *pliohippus*.

By about 30 million years ago, early forms of elephants and hippos lumbered across the plains and rivers of Britain, occasionally bothered by big cats.

Hot and cold

As time passed, Earth's climate underwent constant – but gradual – changes. Every few hundred million years, it started to get very, very cold, and the whole planet entered a period known as an 'ice age'. It was so cold that there was ice covering the north and south poles all year round.

During each ice age, the climate went through gradual hot and cold cycles. Every 100,000 years or so, it grew so cold that vast ice sheets, called glaciers, extended out from the poles to cover large parts of the world, including Britain. These slow hot and cold cycles continue to affect the Earth today.

New life

As the climate changed, the landscape changed, too. Over millions of years, many animals couldn't cope with the changes and died out. But in time new animals, including humans, began to appear.

Building the British Isles

Ever since planet Earth was formed, the land that now makes up the British Isles has experienced freezing, thawing, flooding and all sorts of changes to its landscape, coastline and position on the Earth.

20 million years ago:

The continents of the world as we know them were in roughly the same place as they are today – but the sea levels were very different, and the British Isles weren't islands.

British Isles

Equator

The dark outlines show how the coastline looks today.

450,000 years ago:

Britain and Ireland were connected to each other and to mainland Europe by land 'bridges'.

400,000 years ago:

A period of extreme cold, known as a glaciation, was at its height. Much of Britain was under the ice.

Ice sheet

Where did people come from?

Some of the earliest ancestors of humans – who looked a little like people today – appeared in Africa about 4.5 million years ago. They were ape-like animals called *Australopithecus*, and they walked on two legs.

But, about two million years later, a new kind of early human arrived on the scene. While *Australopithecus* never ventured beyond Africa, these creatures, known as *Homo erectus*, spread out over much of the world, including prehistoric Europe.

People in Britain

A small collection of man-made stone tools, dating back about 750,000 years, has been unearthed near the town of Pakefield in Suffolk. This is the oldest evidence of human life in Britain.

The early humans who left these tools behind were probably descendants of *Homo erectus*. Britain was home to *Homo erectus* for thousands of years. But, about 650,000 years ago, a period of glaciation set in, and the cold drove them all away.

Coming and going

By about 520,000 years ago, the climate had warmed, the ice melted, and a new wave of early humans wandered into Britain. At that time, Britain was a warm place, with a similar climate to today's Mediterranean countries.

But, 70,000 years later, the ice began to come back. People were driven south and away from Britain. This continuous – but gradual – cycle of hot and cold weather meant that early humans settled in Britain, often for thousands of years, at least eight times.

Stone age

At the time the first settlers arrived in Britain, people were making tools from stone.

Prehistorians call this time the Palaeolithic Age, which means 'old stone age'.

This map shows some of the places where settlers in Britain lived about 450,000 years ago.

For much of the Palaeolithic Age, a massive river cut through central Britain. Now known as the River Bytham, it no longer exists.

Hunters and gatherers

Early humans came to Britain following animals. People needed animals to survive. They ate their meat and used their skins for clothes. Instead of living in fixed homes, they followed herds of animals, and slept in makeshift shelters, or inside caves if they were handy.

Many of the creatures they hunted were huge and fierce, and people only had simple tools, such as pointed wooden spears. So they chased animals into bogs or off cliffs, to make killing them easier. More often than hunting, they also scavenged for animals to eat that were already dead.

But the people of this age didn't only eat meat. They also caught fish and gathered shellfish, nuts, fruits and roots. To help with all these tasks, they made themselves tools from wood, bone and stone, and they twisted plant stems and leaves to make rope.

First language

Early humans probably communicated to warn each other when danger was nearby, or to help each other hunt, but they may have relied on body language more than speech.

These hunters have chased a mammoth into a bog, to confuse and exhaust it. They are finishing it off with wooden spears.

Making tools

A small number of animals make simple tools, but only humans know how to make complex tools. Early people made tools from pebbles, especially flint. They also sharpened sticks into deadly spears, and used bones or antlers as hammers.

Handaxes

Prehistoric Britons, from about 500,000 years ago, have left behind many examples of a tool now known as a handaxe. Handaxes were made in different shapes, but were all designed with a round base that fit snugly into a hand, and with a series of sharp edges for cutting.

Handaxes had many uses, but in particular they were used to scrape animal hides, slice meat, and to extract nutritious marrow from bones.

At first, people simply made their own new handaxes whenever they needed one. In time, some people specialized as tool makers, or 'flint knappers', and began to make lots of handaxes to trade for food or other goods.

This flint handaxe, found at Farnham in Surrey, is about 400,000 years old.

Making a handaxe

Here's how archaeologists think people made handaxes:

1. A stone was chosen for its shape, texture and even the sound it made when tapped.

2. A hard hammer stone was used to chip away pieces to make the basic shape.

3. Softer stones, bones and antlers were used to create smaller sharp edges.

New technology

As new settlers came to Britain, they brought new ideas about how to make tools. From about 300,000 years ago, people in parts of Britain began to use a new technique. Instead of making a single tool out of a stone, they hit the stone to break off many small, sharp, chippings. These were perfect to use as knives.

Stone age toolkit

About 200,000 years ago, another new development spread into Britain from Europe. Flint knappers would prepare a 'core' from a suitable stone. By hitting the core in different places, the knapper chipped off flakes of different sizes and shapes. One kind of flake would become a spear tip; another might be a bone saw.

This new method, which has come to be known as the 'Levallois technique', meant that one stone could become a whole toolkit. The technique was used for thousands of years all over Britain and Europe.

Making flakes

Simple flake tools were made by chipping at a stone core.

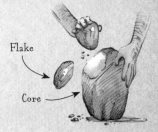

Flake

Core

Flint knappers using the Levallois technique used an antler as a chisel to shape more accurate flakes.

Antler chisel

Stone tools made using the Levallois technique

These tools were used as axeheads about 40,000 years ago.

Made about 20,000 years ago, these were used as sharp knives.

13

All kinds of people

Masters of fire

Homo erectus carefully took burning branches from wild fires to make their own fires.

It may not have been until the time of the Neanderthals that people learned how to start a fire. They banged two rocks together to make a spark, which set light to very dry wood.

This 12,000 year old bone needle is much the same as those *Homo sapiens* would have used 10,000 years earlier.

After the first group of *Homo erectus* came to Britain, at least three different kinds of early humans settled there. First came *Homo heidelbergensis*, who had much bigger brains than *erectus*, made flake tools rather than handaxes, and even made wooden spears.

Then, about 60,000 years ago, came *Homo neanderthalensis*, commonly known as Neanderthals. These humans had even bigger brains, and had learned to cope with cold and snowy weather, although they also lived in warmer parts of southern Europe.

Finally, from about 36,000 years ago, a new kind of human arrived – *Homo sapiens*. These people, who originally came from north Africa, were the ancestors of modern humans.

Homo sapiens were taller and thinner than Neanderthals, and they had smaller brains – although this didn't necessarily mean they were less intelligent. Both kinds of people talked, used tools, and even knew how to build elaborate traps to capture large animals.

Keeping out the cold

Neanderthals lived through at least two major glacial periods. Perhaps their most useful invention for surviving harsh winters was clothing.

To make clothes, Neanderthals took leather hides and carefully scraped them clean. Then they heated the hides over a fire, to make them softer, so they could be shaped. They also used strips of leather to make belts.

Homo sapiens added another vital step to clothing technology. They punched holes into animal hides, and used needles made of bone, and thread made from thin strips of leather to sew hides together. These well-fitting clothes were much warmer than loose hides.

This is a Neanderthal skeleton in a grave. Neanderthals often placed their dead in this way, with the knees tucked up in a sleeping position.

Respect for the dead

Neanderthals and *Homo sapiens* were some of the earliest people to carry out rituals – ceremonies to mark out special occasions in their lives. No one knows if they performed weddings, but they did have funerals.

Neanderthals buried their dead in graves. *Homo sapiens* took their rituals even further: they buried precious objects in the graves of their loved ones.

Where did the Neanderthals go?

Neanderthals disappeared from Britain around 30,000 years ago. Shortly after that, they disappeared altogether.

No one knows exactly why the Neanderthals died out. Some experts think there's a rather sinister explanation – that *Homo sapiens* gradually killed them all. They may have killed them in combat, or perhaps they drove them off into areas where there was little food and shelter.

Family tree

Today, there is only one kind of human on Earth – *Homo sapiens*. This family tree shows the link between the early humans that are thought to have lived in Britain, and when they existed.

Homo erectus
(1.8 million – 500,000 years ago)

Homo heidelbergensis
(600,000 – 200,000 years ago)

Homo neanderthalensis
(250,000 - 30,000 years ago)

Homo sapiens
(200,000 years ago - present day)

The first artists

Artist's materials

Paints were made from charcoal to get black, earth for shades of brown, and rocks and certain plants for red, orange and yellow.

This carving of a stag is about 13,000 years old. It comes from Creswell Crags in Derbyshire, and is the oldest cave art found in Britain so far.

Early Britons didn't spend all their time worrying about food, shelter and basic survival. They devoted a lot of time and effort to creating art and enjoying their social lives, just as people do today.

It's certain that once *Homo sapiens* arrived, art was everywhere, but earlier humans may have decorated their bodies and homes in some way, too.

Cave art

Some of the most spectacular art from this time can still be seen today. It's found on the walls and floors of caves. Carvings and paintings show all kinds of animals, especially the ones people hunted and ate, such as horses, deer and bison.

No one knows whether such artwork had a special meaning, but it's possible that it was intended to bring hunters good luck. Many cave paintings were made on top of old pictures, so it's likely the act of creating art was considered as important as the picture itself.

A pale line has been added to this photo to make the carved outline of the stag easier to see.

Carvings and ornaments

While some prehistoric artists were carving pictures onto walls, others made models and ornaments. People painted pebbles, or carved stones and pieces of bone to make beautiful objects, such as miniature animals. They used shells and small bones to make necklaces and other accessories.

Decorated skeleton

A grave found in Paviland Cave, in South Wales, revealed a man who was buried around 26,000 years ago. His body – or perhaps his clothes – had been decorated all over with a kind of powder called red ochre. He was also wearing a necklace made of sea shells, and ivory bracelets. These sorts of ornaments may have been typical of a burial at this time. But archaeologists think it's more likely this man was a tribal chief, or a religious leader.

Art trade

Homo sapiens were great inventors. They designed and made all sorts of tools to make art with. One tool in particular was very common at the end of the Palaeolithic Age: a hooked, pointed stick called a burin. It was used to engrave markings into pieces of bone.

Works of art became some of the earliest examples of trade between communities. People from different families exchanged them, perhaps to buy food or tools, or else they gave them as gifts.

Ancient carvings of humans and animals have been found all over Europe. Some of these carvings were passed between people along ancient trade routes that spread for many thousands of miles.

Music

Prehistoric craftsmen fashioned musical instruments, such as flutes, from wood and bone.

Bone carving

This bone object is known as a baton. Many batons have been dug up, but no one knows what they were for.

Batons have notches down the side, which experts think may have marked out periods of time, such as months or weeks.

After the ice

Believe it or not, the world is still experiencing an ice age today. Ice still covers the north and south poles, but the last time it covered the British Isles was between about 18,000 and 16,000 years ago. At that time, it was too cold for people or animals to survive there.

From about 16,000 years ago, the ice began to retreat. And by about 14,700 years ago, new settlers came to stay. There have been people living in Britain ever since.

This scene shows a campsite near a river. People are collecting fish and shellfish, hunting animals and gathering berries and nuts. Hunter-gatherers returned to sites like this year after year.

New best friend

During this period, people learned how to domesticate dogs. Bred from wolves, farmers kept them to assist with herding, or possibly even to guard communities against invaders.

Seasonal movers

About 12,000 years ago, a long period of warm weather began, and this encouraged a wide variety of plants and trees to grow. People didn't have to travel very far to collect what they needed, or to find herds of animals to hunt. Every year they moved between just a few campsites, according to the season, choosing places where they would have plenty to eat at that time of year.

Hunting equipment

Around this time, hunters developed more advanced techniques and tools. They had bows and arrows, probably for killing birds. The arrowheads were made from incredibly sharp, fingernail-sized flakes of stone, known as microliths.

They also invented a device (see right), which enabled them to hurl their spears as far as 250m (275 yards). Hunters in some parts of the world still use similar spear throwers today.

Spear thrower

handle groove

This hunter has fitted his spear into the groove at the back of the thrower. He swings his arm...

...and the spear flies out of the thrower, and into the distance.

A new age

As the population of Britain was becoming more settled, a new age was dawning. Prehistorians call it the Mesolithic Age, or 'middle stone age'. This period began about 10,000 years ago, in 8000BC.

Groups of people at this time were still moving from one place to another as the seasons changed. But in their seasonal camps, they were getting better at building long-term shelters, made from wood and animal skins, that they could return to year after year.

Britain BC

To describe dates from prehistoric times, the letters BC are often used. This means the dates are from before the birth of Christ, over 2,000 years ago.

Dates from this period are counted backwards. So, the bigger the number BC, the longer ago it is.

Marking out territory

It's likely that there were more people in Britain at this time than ever before, living not just in family groups, but as small communities. As well as building shelters, these Mesolithic communities cleared away trees to mark out their territory. They also burned down trees to make clearings in the forests. Bands of hunters lured herds of animals into these clearings to make it easier to pick them off with bows and arrows.

This is a reconstruction of the oldest house ever found in Britain, known today as Howick House. The original house was built in 7850BC, on the coast of Northumberland.

Doggerland

Ireland became separated from the mainland during the early Mesolithic Age, but Britain was not yet an island. To the east, a vast area of land, known as 'Doggerland', connected Britain to lands as far north as modern-day Denmark.

In 8000BC, Doggerland was a lush place, home to many people. But over the next thousand years, the seas rose and Doggerland slowly became an island. Eventually, this island disappeared altogether under the swelling North Sea.

North Sea

Denmark

Doggerland

Britain

English Channel

This map shows how part of northern Europe looked in around 8000BC. The dark outline shows land as it is today.

All at sea

At this time, one of best sources of food was the sea. Mesolithic Britons wove nets and baskets to collect fish and especially shellfish. They also fashioned tiny flint fishing hooks, and made big, spiky harpoons for catching larger fish.

Mesolithic fishermen hollowed out logs to make canoes. They paddled up rivers or along the coast to find new fishing grounds, or new sources of flint. Canoes also made it easier for some communities to meet and trade with each other.

During the Mesolithic Age, settlers arrived to stay in Ireland for the first time, probably making their way by boat from southwest Scotland. These early settlers lived along the coast; inland Ireland at this time was a barren, icy wasteland.

Mesolithic hunters went fishing in rivers or along the coast, hoping to catch big fish with bone harpoons.

This deer skull, dating back to around 7500BC, was found in Star Carr in Yorkshire. The two round holes were cut into the skull so a person could attach it to his head using leather straps.

Rituals

Just like people today, Mesolithic Britons played music, danced, sang songs, and performed rituals. Experts may never know exactly what religious beliefs these people held, but they do know that death and animals played a major part.

Hunting Masks

These hunters are wearing masks and animal skins.

Experts don't know if this is how people dressed to hunt deer, but it's one explanation of finds such as the Star Carr skull.

Hunting magic

Although people found most of their food by fishing and collecting berries and nuts, meat was prized above all. So it was animals, and the act of hunting, that fired people's imaginations.

In some places, people collected the skulls of animals they had killed. Hunters may even have worn these skulls as masks, possibly as part of their hunting costume, or perhaps priests wore them during a ritual to bless a hunt.

The cannibals of Gough's Cave

Mesolithic Britons didn't only eat meat from animals – some of them were cannibals, too. Human remains found in Gough's Cave in Somerset from over 14,000 years ago show that eyeballs were gouged out of their sockets, skulls were cut open, and marrow was sucked from the bones.

Perhaps these cannibals performed a human sacrifice first – killing a person as part of a ritual – and then ate the bodies. Or perhaps they ate them as part of a funeral rite after a person died naturally.

Ritual eating of the dead may have symbolized the belief that an ancestor's spirit would live on. Or people may have believed that eating the remains of a successful hunter would pass on his skill.

Some people may have killed enemies and eaten them to scare off rivals. And it's possible that, from time to time, they resorted to eating each other simply because food was very scarce.

This is the skull of 'Cheddar Man', who died in about 7150BC, and was discovered in Gough's Cave. There are some small holes in this skull which were made by people cutting out the brain, possibly to eat it.

Life and death

Archaeologists have uncovered very few burials from Mesolithic Britain. Because graves from this period are so rare, experts think most people cremated their dead relatives, or left their bodies out, probably in sacred places, to be eaten by animals.

A number of bodies have been found among piles of old sea shells, known as middens. Were these the bodies of hated enemies or criminals thrown out with the trash, or was this a way to commemorate the death of a beloved friend? Either way, it's likely that the way a person lived was reflected in the way their relatives chose to mark their death.

Local ties

Using DNA found in the bones of 9,000 year old Cheddar Man, experts have traced his family tree to the present day.

Among his many descendants is school teacher Adrian Target, who still lives in Cheddar village.

Early farmers

One of the most significant developments in the whole of human history was the invention of farming. People first tried out various ways of farming around 11,000 years ago, in the Middle East.

Over the next few thousand years, farming know-how – and farmers themselves – spread through Europe. People learned how to grow enough food to feed themselves, their families, and their herds. Successful crop growers found they could sustain bigger families than ever before, and the population of Europe, including Britain, gradually increased.

Farming skills, and in particular the tools used for farming, marked the start of a new period of prehistory, known as the Neolithic Age.

New stone age

Prehistorians call the period between about 4000BC and 2500BC the Neolithic Age, or 'new stone age'.

People still made their tools from stone, but now they used stone grinders to shape and polish them.

These stone tools belonged to Neolithic farmers in Britain. They are around 5,000 years old.

This curved blade was used to harvest crops.

These two stone axes would each have had a wooden handle.

Axes like these would have been used for chopping wood and as weapons.

Farming in Britain

The first farms appeared in Britain around 4000BC. For many years, farmers came and went from mainland Europe, in boats filled with sheep and cows. Some brought seeds to grow crops such as wheat and barley, along with farming tools for digging the soil and harvesting. They settled and set up their own farms, or traded with locals.

For a time, some people continued to live by hunting wild animals and gathering fruits and nuts. But, during the Neolithic Age, farming became the most common way of life throughout Britain. Wild boar, which had long been hunted in Britain's forests, were tamed and eventually farmed as pigs. Hunting remained popular, but only as a seasonal activity, or perhaps as a ritual, or even a pastime.

Changing the landscape

Over the next thousand years, farmers cut down great swathes of woodland to make space to grow crops and graze herds. It was a laborious job; the trees were felled using polished stone axes, and the dead wood was taken away and burned.

Eventually, lush forests turned into wide expanses of grassland used for animals to graze on, or cultivated by cropgrowers. Some farms were very successful. Their owners showed off their wealth off by sacrificing, feasting on and even burying hundreds of cattle.

Communities worked together to build great monuments. Massive, imposing tombs were erected, made of vast mounds of earth, or stones piled on top of each other. They may have represented a religious belief, as well as standing for a community's ownership of the land.

Hard work

Farming was much more time-consuming than hunting. One endless job was grinding wheat into flour, using a pair of stones called 'quern stones'.

From wear and tear found on their spines, experts believe that it was Neolithic women who did this almost back-breaking task.

These huge stone slabs, close to the east coast of Ireland, were set up by early farmers to mark the place where their dead ancestors were buried.

Firm footing

Early farmers built long trackways to cross marshy ground. Some may have looked like this one, made from split tree trunks supported on smaller wooden posts.

One trackway found in Somerset, in southern England, ran for almost 2km (over a mile).

Homes and communities

As people took to farming, they no longer had to travel to find food. So, while some families continued to move around and set up seasonal camps, many others began to settle and form fixed communities.

These first settlements were surrounded by rough plots of land, used for growing crops and grazing animals. Initially, farmers didn't set up fields with well-marked boundaries; they simply used the land where they lived.

In time, Neolithic people built small houses, using timber or stone. A family of up to twelve would live in a simple, rectangular, one-roomed house, which remained habitable for generations.

This is the remains of a workshop in Skara Brae in the Orkney Islands – a rare example of a Neolithic village. It was inhabited from about 3100BC – 2500BC.

Kiln

Shelves for storage and display (see page 29)

Fireplace

Alcove

Gathering places

As well as building farms and houses, local people in many parts of Britain got together to create communal spaces, of at least the size of a football pitch, marked out by a series of ditches and earth mounds.

These places are now known as 'causewayed enclosures'. Some people may have lived inside them, but they were probably mostly used for ceremonies, such as weddings and funerals. They may also have been used as a place where people could seek safety from attackers, and, if the enclosures were big enough, where cattle could be kept protected from raiders.

Some families, or groups of families, lived in long, wooden houses. These dwellings were common in Neolithic Europe, but only a few examples have been found in Britain.

Originally, the workshop had a roof made of thick moss, held up by beams made of whale bone or wood. This kept out the cold north wind.

Fun and games

Neolithic times weren't all about hard work on the farm. These small blocks found in Skara Brae are some of the oldest dice in Britain.

Mining and craft

Neolithic people made tools from stone and bone, often fixed onto wooden handles. The best quality stones, such as flint, weren't found everywhere, so some communities set up mines so they could exchange their local flint for other goods they didn't have.

Grimes Graves

One of the most productive flint mines in Britain was Grimes Graves, in East Anglia. The oldest mine shaft there was dug in around 3000BC. Over the next 2,000 years, over 430 more shafts were dug, using picks made from antlers, and shovels made from ox bones.

In some mines, people set aside one shaft as a shrine, perhaps to make offerings to the gods so that the mine would yield good stones, or possibly to ask them for protection. The mines would have been dark, frightening and dangerous places to work.

Axes for everyone

The most common tools found from the Neolithic Age are axes, which were used to cut down trees.

It also became fashionable to own axes made of carefully polished precious stones, such as jade or jet, that were never used to chop anything. Some of the finest ornamental axes in Britain came from Pike of Stickle, a mountain in the Lake District in the northeast of England.

Many stone objects came from faraway places, even from beyond Britain. It's likely that powerful people sought them to show off how wealthy and well-connected they were.

Miners at Grimes Graves were able to dig shafts over 15m (50 ft) deep. They used wooden ladders to get up and down.

Some seams of flint were dug out of the walls of each shaft, but the most valued flint, known as floorstone, was found at the bottom.

Visitors to Grimes Graves today can climb to the bottom of one of the surviving shafts.

Potmakers

Stonemasons were not the only craftsmen in Neolithic Britain. Traders and settlers from Europe introduced a new skill to the islands: pottery. People used clay to shape different styles of pot, for cooking or storing food. Then they fired – or baked them hard – on open fires.

Carpenters

Carpentry was also spreading through most communities. As well as building houses and other structures, carpenters from this period also made all sorts of fine carved household objects, including wooden bowls, axe handles, and even figurines.

Practical pots

Now that people were making pottery jars and bowls, it was easier for them to store food. They could also cook new types of food, such as porridge.

Status symbols

Ornamental objects, such as the ones shown below, were prized possessions. Many have been found in large community tombs, or buried in sacred parts of the land.

These stone cylinders are known as the 'Folkton drums'. Etched onto the sides are three of the oldest representations of faces found in Britain.

These carved stone balls, found on a set of shelves at Skara Brae, are each about as big as an apple. Decorative objects like these have been found all over Neolithic Scotland.

This 20cm (8in) long axehead is made of polished jade. It was found in Britain but originally crafted in the Italian Alps.

Mysterious monuments

Neolithic people in the British Isles spent many years building monuments that are still standing today, over 5,000 years since they were made. There are a few clues as to why people built these vast structures, but much about them is still shrouded in mystery.

Underground tombs

In around 3200BC, before the pyramids in Egypt were built, work began on an underground tomb now known as Newgrange, by the River Boyne in eastern Ireland. Similar tombs were later built in other parts of Neolithic Britain.

From the outside, Newgrange consists of a large circular wall, and covered with a mound of clay and grass. Inside, a stone passage slopes up, leading to a central burial chamber, with three smaller chambers around it.

Every year at dawn on the shortest day (the winter solstice), a beam of sunlight shines through an opening above the entrance, and lights up the main chamber. Achieving this was a remarkable feat of design.

Art gallery

The stone walls inside the tomb at Newgrange are covered in swirling circular patterns – a typical feature of Neolithic art.

Sunlight shines into the central chamber at Newgrange.

Sun

Central chamber

Entrance

This is Newgrange as it looks today. The outer wall has been substantially reconstructed to show how it first looked.

Mounds and henges

Not all monuments were as grand as Newgrange. Simple ones were made by digging ditches or piling up earth into mounds. Sometimes people built a tall, round mound that looked like a hill. Other mounds were very long, often 60m (66 yards) or more. These long mounds may have set out the routes for ceremonial processions.

Around 3000BC, people in many regions began to build 'henges'. These were big, upright timbers or stones fixed into the ground, and arranged in circles or lines. Sometimes, other big stones or timbers were laid flat on top of the uprights.

By far the biggest henge was built at Avebury in south west England. An outer stone circle stretched over 335m (366 yards) across. Two smaller separate circles were later added inside it.

What were they for?

Ancient farmers may have made monuments to mark out their territory. And many mounds, known as barrows, were used as burial places – usually for whole communities, not just individual people.

Some may also have been built to celebrate the changing seasons. Like Newgrange, many monuments were designed so that particular parts of them lined up to catch the sunlight at midwinter or midsummer.

Mighty mound

Silbury Hill, in Wiltshire, is an earth monument built around 4,500 years ago. Many similar prehistoric mounds have been found across Europe, but this is the biggest.

To make a mound this vast, some 500 people would have had to work every day for 10 years.

Archaeologists have excavated parts of the hill to see if it hid an important burial, but nothing has been found inside.

Stonehenge

Standing proud on Salisbury Plain is one of the most
famous prehistoric sites in Britain: Stonehenge. It's one
of a dozen monuments within a day's walk of each other,
which were in use for nearly 1,500 years.

The oldest of these is a long mound, built in around
3600BC. Later, a number of barrows were put up nearby.
The area became a place for burials and other rituals,
and, within it, any farming, hunting or fighting was
probably forbidden. In about 3200BC, work began on a
new monument, that would become Stonehenge.

Mysterious holes

The oldest version of Stonehenge didn't have any
stones in it at all. It was a circular ditch enclosing a
series of raised earth banks. There probably weren't
any structures built on top of these banks, but several
small holes were dug in a circle just inside the
enclosure. No one knows what these were
used for at this time.

Woodhenge

Just a short walk away
from the stone circle at
Stonehenge, is
'Woodhenge' – a smaller
double circle of standing
wooden posts.

It may have been a
place where animals, and
sometimes even humans,
were sacrificed.

Stonehenge was in
use from around
3200BC to about
1500BC, although
different
generations of
people probably used
it differently.

Sticks and stones

The first stones in the monument were erected sometime around 3000BC. Shortly after that, the banks inside the henge were raised, and a wooden structure of some kind was built on top. People began to use the small holes as places to bury cremated human remains.

The end of a journey

In the years after 3000BC, a great avenue was created, leading up from the River Avon to Stonehenge. Near the start of this avenue, a new stone circle, known today as Bluehenge, was put up.

A century or so later, the Bluehenge stones were moved inside Stonehenge, and later arranged into a horseshoe shape.

Some experts believe people carried the dead along the River Avon and then processed up to Stonehenge as part of a funeral, before burying the bodies elsewhere. But others think healing ceremonies were held here.

Raising the stones

To make the outer wall at Stonehenge, people used ropes to raise a series of upright slabs. Each upright had two bumps on top.

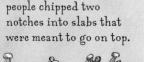

Using balls of hard stone, people chipped two notches into slabs that were meant to go on top.

Then, these top slabs were lifted into position using timber frames and levers.

One notch of the top stone fit onto a bump on one upright, the other notch fit onto a bump on the next upright slab in the circle.

The Bronze Age

Metalworking

To make things from bronze, Bronze Age metalworkers found rocks containing the metals tin and copper.

They crushed the rocks and then heated them over a fire until the metals in the rocks melted – a process called smelting.

Next, metalworkers poured the molten metal mixture into specially shaped hollows carved into pieces of stone or clay.

After the metal had cooled a little, it could be hammered into different shapes, and decorations could be added.

From about 2500BC, a new discovery changed people's lives all over Europe – how to make things out of metal. People first learned how to shape copper to make small blades and ornaments. Soon after that, they were working with tin and gold. By about 2150BC, they discovered how to make bronze – a mixture of copper and tin.

The period that began with the discovery of metalwork is now known as the Bronze Age, even though bronze itself was not the first metal made.

These two Bronze Age copper knife blades originally had wooden handles, which have rotted away over the centuries.

A handle would have been attached here.

Some experts refer to the early Bronze Age as the 'Copper Age', because most metal objects found from this time were made from copper.

Digging for bronze

Some parts of Britain had plentiful sources of copper and tin. They were used separately to make everyday tools. Skilled metalworkers combined them to make valuable bronze ornaments.

Vast copper mines were dug at Great Orme in Wales, and Ross Island and Mount Gabriel in Ireland. Tin was found in Cornwall. Like the great stone mines, many were in continuous use for thousands of years.

This solid gold
cape was found
in a Bronze Age
burial at Mold in
North Wales.

It must have
restricted arm
movements
a lot, so was
probably
only worn on
very special
occasions.

Powerful chiefs

People who controlled metal mines and metalworking
forges became rich and powerful. These wealthy
individuals were perhaps the earliest chiefs in Britain,
ruling over a few farmsteads or large villages. They
probably held onto their power by force, although
experts believe this was a relatively peaceful period.

They acquired beautiful objects made of gold and
bronze, often from thousands of miles away, to display
their status as chiefs.

Gift giving

In those days, money didn't exist. Instead, people used
their possessions to display their wealth, and as a way
of bargaining with others. Sometimes, they would give
away some of their possessions as 'gifts'.

If one chief gave a gift – say, a large amount of
copper – to a rival chief, it meant he could expect to be
repaid in the future. This might involve an offer of help
to build a henge, or a share of the next harvest, or just a
promise not to attack.

This is a bronze bracelet
from 1400 BC, in a style
known as 'Sussex loop'.
Accessories in this style
are unique to the
Brighton area.

Originally, this
bracelet was shiny bronze,
but over the ages it has
tarnished, giving it a dull
green appearance.

The Amesbury Archer

Life after death

Archaeologists think that Bronze Age people believed in an afterlife. They buried their dead with items that they needed to take with them.

In 2002, archaeologists unearthed the richest Bronze Age burial yet found in Britain. The grave, uncovered in Amesbury near Stonehenge, contained the body of a 40 year-old man, who had died in around 2300BC.

He was surrounded by a variety of objects, including a bow and arrows – so the man has come to be known as the Amesbury Archer. The sheer number of items, as well as their high quality, shows he was something of a local celebrity. In fact, analysis of his remains has shown that he grew up in the Swiss Alps.

At the time of the Amesbury Archer, a new culture, now known as Beaker Culture, was spreading throughout western Europe. The Amesbury Archer was perhaps one of the first people to bring this new culture to Britain.

The Amesbury Archer was buried with a particularly lavish set of objects, arranged carefully around his body. Many of them were put into bags which have rotted away.

Prize items included two gold hair ornaments and 16 flint arrowheads.

Beakers and metals

Beaker Culture gets its name from a new style of decorated pot that was widely used in early Bronze Age Europe. Beakers were so cherished that most important people were buried with at least one. The Amesbury Archer was buried with four.

Beakers were made from clay, and were decorated with patterns of lines. Some beakers were used to drink a popular new alcoholic drink made from honey, called mead. Others were used for smelting metals or as burial urns.

Beaker Culture wasn't only about pottery. Working with metals and using metal objects was important, too. People in Britain only began to make and trade metal items after Beaker Culture arrived, in about 2400BC. Some early metal goods came to Britain from as far away as Greece.

Meeting and eating

Beaker Culture thrived in Britain for about 500 years. During this time a number of great building projects were completed, including the stone circles at Stonehenge.

At special times of year, whole communities met up at some of the bigger outdoor monuments, such as Avebury. They celebrated and worshipped together, exchanged gifts and enjoyed a great feast. Feasts provided an opportunity for chiefs to display their wealth, for example by sacrificing, eating and even burying whole herds of cows or pigs.

This beaker was found in a grave in Bedfordshire. Perhaps it was intended to be used in a great feast in the afterlife.

Burial mounds

During the Neolithic Age, people had buried their dead in large groups, beneath long mounds or stone monuments. But people in the Early Bronze Age preferred to bury individuals under smaller, round barrows. In some places, they built rows of barrows to commemorate generations of important people.

This row of barrows in Dorset can still be seen today.

These Bronze Age warriors have just raided a rival settlement.

Clashing communities

As the centuries passed, Beaker Culture faded away, and life in Britain became more hostile. It became fashionable for chiefs to show off their power by wearing ever more lavish gold ornaments, and by displaying lots of ornate spears, swords and shields. These were not usually used for fighting, but anyone who could afford them could clearly afford plenty of working weapons, too.

These new riches also bred new conflicts, as different groups tried to grab more wealth, status and territory for themselves.

Sheltered housing

Instead of building monuments, people began to create defensive enclosures to keep out raiders from rival groups. Some covered whole hilltops, but others protected the homes of just a few families. People farmed in fields outside the enclosures, but stored their crops in pits within them, and herded their animals inside when their farms were under attack.

This thick bronze shield dates back to about 1000BC. It was big enough to protect a person who crouched down behind it.

38

The French connection

One of the most spectacular finds from
the mid Bronze Age is the Dover Boat,
a wooden trading vessel which was built
in around 1550BC. It was used to ferry goods,
including bronze, and groups of people, across the
English Channel.

Around this time, people in the south of Britain
shared many more cultural similarities with people in
France than they did with those who lived in the north
of Britain. It's likely they even shared a language.

The Dover Boat was
originally nearly 18m
(60ft) long, and needed
at least nine pairs of
paddlers to power it. Its
cargo included goods
such as scrap metal.

Horse power

Experts don't know when horses were first tamed, but
they became very important during the Bronze Age. At
first, people used horse-drawn carts to transport heavy
goods and, sometimes, important people, too. But later,
rich warriors began to use horses in battle.

Warriors would charge forward standing on chariots
drawn by two horses, creating panic among enemy
footsoldiers. Then they would leap off
to join the fray on foot.

This huge chalk horse
stretches 110m (375ft)
across a hill near
Uffington in western
England. It may have
been carved as long ago
as 1400BC.

Fashion show

Scraps of clothing and grooming tools found in marshy places give experts an idea of the fashions of the time.

Men and women all wore hats, and skirts with tunics, although men's skirts were shorter. The men were clean-shaven.

The marshes at Flag Fen can have a ghostly atmosphere. Perhaps Bronze Age priests used this to help mourners imagine dead relatives passing from the world of the living to the land of the dead.

Cold and wet

Europe was a warm and lush place in the Early Bronze Age. But a change in the weather was on its way.

By about 850BC, a long period of cold temperatures and heavy rainfall left farmers struggling to grow the crops they had previously relied on. Many of the once-fertile fields were abandoned because they were no longer producing good harvests. In time, these places would become heaths and moors.

Flag Fen

Life in Britain didn't come to a standstill, though. Communities simply changed the way they lived, and moved into new kinds of settlements.

One Late Bronze Age site, at a place called Flag Fen in Cambridgeshire, has revealed lots of fascinating finds. It's clear that people lived and farmed here but, perhaps more importantly, Flag Fen was a religious place. At its heart was a long wooden track across a marsh, which once connected two settlements. People gathered along the trackway to deposit things into the water as part of a ritual.

Going underground

From the Mid Bronze Age – even before the weather turned – people all over Britain had begun to place objects in marshes and rivers, or to bury them in the earth. These objects ranged from ornate swords and ornaments to simple pots.

    The great number of objects found in places such as Flag Fen, and the careful way most of them were placed, suggest that people weren't throwing them away. Instead, it's thought these were some sort of prayer offerings, perhaps to ask the gods for a good harvest, or a happy home, or success in battle.

A dark age

Little is known about how people lived between about 800BC and 300BC. Once-thriving mines shut down, and people stopped burying their dead, or even preserving burned remains in urns. People even seem to have stopped using bronze or other metals. Life, work and art must have continued, but not in a form that survives today.

The Iron Age

During the Late Bronze Age, the first iron objects appeared in Britain. But it wasn't until about 800BC that Britons were able to make their own tools and weapons from this metal.

Rocks containing iron were much easier to find than those containing copper and tin, and iron is a tougher metal than bronze. But extracting and working iron is more difficult – it requires extremely hot furnaces to melt the rocks, and repeated heating and hammering to remove impurities from the iron.

A growing population

Iron tools brought about a farming boom. People were able to clear more forests than ever before, creating new farmland, and farmers were able to dig into heavier soils and plant more crops. This enabled Iron Age Britons to grow more food than before, leading to a rise in the population. It's estimated that, during the Iron Age, the number of people in Britain went from under a million to two million, or even more.

Hillforts

People continued to build fortified enclosures on hilltops, but these were often larger and more complex than earlier Bronze Age ones had been. Now known as hillforts, they were surrounded by rings of defensive ditches and earth banks.

During the Iron Age, thousands of these new hillforts were built all over Britain. The remains of the ditches and banks around many of them can be seen today, although very few of the structures that used to be on top have survived.

Ironmasters

This is part of an iron 'firedog' from Capel Garmon in Wales. It was made in about 50BC. Firedogs were probably placed in pairs on either side of a hearth, most likely as decoration.

It took great skill to make this kind of ornate object. The earliest iron workers were believed to possess a magical gift.

Two pairs of firedogs are shown in position around a fire.

42

Hillfort life

Hillforts served many different purposes. Some were fortified villages, large enough for lots of people to live inside. Others were only used when people in surrounding settlements needed a place of refuge in times of war.

Many hillforts were probably also used for trading, or as spaces where religious ceremonies were conducted. Others may have been built to display the power and wealth of the tribes who built them.

Inside those hillforts where people lived, they had almost everything they needed. There were round houses with thatched roofs, barns for keeping animals in or storing food, workshops for making iron tools and weapons, and places to set up market stalls.

King of castles

By around 800BC, Maiden Castle in Dorset, in the south of England, had become one of the biggest hillforts in Europe.

This photograph shows Maiden Castle as it looks today. The rings of earth around the hillside were once topped with stout wooden fences known as palisades.

A family of tribes

The people of Iron Age Europe are sometimes referred to as the Celts. The Celts shared similar languages, religions and culture, but they weren't really one group of people. They lived in separate communities, or tribes, each with its own ruler and traditions. Each tribe was made up of smaller groups, known as clans, which were a little like extended families.

Much of what we know about life in Iron Age Britain comes from records kept by Ancient Greek and Roman writers. They encountered the Britons on their travels, and through trading with them. Seeing similarities between tribes in Britain and tribes across Europe, they described all these people as 'Celts'.

This is the front and back of a coin from the late Iron Age, bearing the name Tincomarus, a chief from southern England.

Iron Age Britons began making and using coins in the 1st century BC, copying the Romans and other Europeans.

At home

Britain still didn't have any towns or cities. Instead, people lived in small settlements or individual farms, with a single-roomed, circular house known as roundhouse for each family.

Roundhouses had wooden frames and outer walls made from willow branches, plastered with a mixture of earth and straw, known as wattle and daub. The roof was cone-shaped and thatched with straw or reeds stetching almost to the ground.

This picture shows a typical Iron Age roundhouse. Part of the roof has been cut away to show the interior.

Arts and crafts

A lot of superbly crafted artwork has survived from the Iron Age. Artists and craftspeople decorated their pottery, metalwork and ornaments with animal designs, or with elaborate patterns made up of curves and spirals. They also made all sorts of accessories, including brooches and thick neck rings known as torcs, made from twisted strands of gold and silver wire.

This beautiful example of British metalwork shows the back of a mirror, covered in swirling Celtic designs. The other side would have been highly polished to create a reflective surface.

Traders

Iron Age Britons traded with people from all over mainland Europe. Ships arrived regularly from as far away as the Mediterranean. They brought fine pottery, wine, oil, glassware and coins to exchange for British goods such as tin and lead, grain, wool and animal skins.

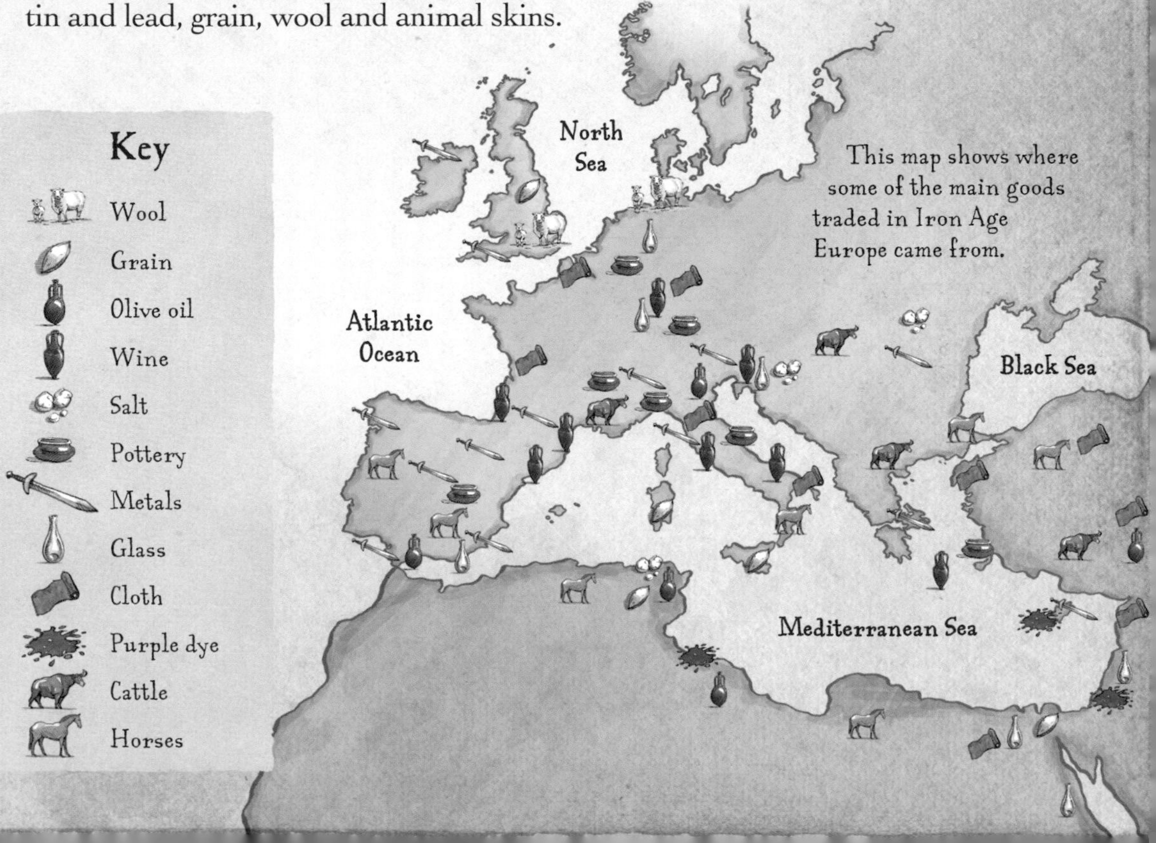

North Sea

This map shows where some of the main goods traded in Iron Age Europe came from.

Atlantic Ocean

Black Sea

Mediterranean Sea

Key

- Wool
- Grain
- Olive oil
- Wine
- Salt
- Pottery
- Metals
- Glass
- Cloth
- Purple dye
- Cattle
- Horses

Homes and shelters

Iron Age Britons built roundhouses and hillforts all over the area that is now England, especially in the south and west. But in Scotland and Ireland people constructed other types of buildings, too: brochs, wheelhouses and crannogs. Some were family homes, some fortified settlements, while others were used as shelters for cattle and sheep.

This is how a broch might have looked. Part of the outer wall has been removed so you can see the different floors inside it.

Stone towers

A number of round stone towers, known as brochs, have been found in Scotland, particularly in the north west. Most had thick walls, and some were up to 15m (45ft) high – tall enough to have up to four floors. The walls were built of large stones, stacked up without any mortar holding them together. The floors inside the broch were joined by a staircase that ran between the outer wall and a thinner inner wall. Each floor had one or more small rooms or 'cells'.

Some brochs were used as houses, but others may have been forts where local farmers went to hide when raiders were in the area. Many brochs were built near the coast, on hilltops or the edges of cliffs, where they could be seen from miles away.

Radiating rooms

Also unique to Scotland was a building called a wheelhouse. Wheelhouses got their name because they were laid out in the shape of a wheel. In the middle was a circular space for a hearth. Stone walls radiated from here to the outer walls, like spokes of a wheel.

These walls created separate rooms which were occupied by different families, or members of a large family. In some places, wheelhouses were dug into the ground, so that only the roofs would have been visible from outside.

This drawing shows the layout of a typical wheelhouse. There was a communal area in the middle, where people gathered around a fire.

Island settlements

The remains of Iron Age crannogs have been found in lakes all over Scotland and Ireland. Crannogs were man-made islands built of stones and wooden posts. Each would have had one or more roundhouses built on top, often surrounded by a wooden fence. Crannogs could only be reached by boat or by crossing a narrow causeway, so they were difficult places to attack.

Archaeologists have reconstructed this crannog at Loch Tay in Scotland, based on remains found there.

Roman writings describe a number of religious festivals held in Britain at important times in the farming year. These are the four main ones:

Imbolc, in February, celebrated the birth of the first lambs, and the arrival of spring.

Beltane, in May, marked the time when the cattle were taken to their summer pastures.

Lugnasad, in August, celebrated the ripening of the crops.

Samhain, in November, marked the end of one year and the beginning of the next with huge bonfires.

Death and religion

Iron Age Britons didn't build monuments or temples. But, like the people of the late Bronze Age, they left hundreds and thousands of offerings buried in the ground, or placed in lakes, streams or bogs.

From these finds, and from Roman writings of the time, it seems that the people of Iron Age Britain worshipped many gods and spirits that were probably linked to parts of the natural world, such as rocks, trees, lakes or bogs.

Mysterious Druids

According to Roman writers, Celtic religious ceremonies were organized by people called Druids. These priest-like figures were said to train for several years, learning how to conduct rituals correctly, and how to prepare medicines from herbs.

This knowledge was passed on by word of mouth, and kept secret from anyone who wasn't a Druid. Very little is known about these people, but they may have been political leaders as well as priests.

The Romans were suspicious of the Druids and the influence they held in Celtic society. In the year 61, Roman soldiers attacked a Druid stronghold on the island of Anglesey in Wales, killing many.

Human sacrifice

One of the grizzliest Celtic rituals the Romans wrote about was human sacrifice. In fact, a number of Iron Age bodies have been discovered in bogs, bearing signs of violent deaths. They may have been chosen by Druids to be sacrificed. You can find out more about these bog bodies on page 52.

A chariot burial at Wetwang

Most Iron Age tribes in Britain didn't bury their dead. But one tribe in East Yorkshire buried chiefs and nobles with all sorts of goods, sometimes including a chariot. One of these graves, uncovered in 2001 near the village of Wetwang, contains the body of a woman who died in around 300BC. It's likely she was a respected leader, and perhaps a warrior, too. Her funeral may have happened like this:

1. Members of the tribe processed to the grave site, carrying her body on a chariot she had used in life.

2. A great feast was laid on. Choice cuts of meat were set aside, some to offer to the gods, others kept for the burial.

3. At the grave itself, they laid her body on its side, placing the meat and a finely decorated iron mirror beside her.

4. Next, they dismantled the chariot, and buried the wheels and harnessing equipment for horses.

5. Then, they laid the base of the chariot on top of the body. Perhaps she was hoping to ride it in the afterlife. Finally, the grave was covered over with earth.

These are two pieces from an Iron Age horse's harness of the type found in chariot burials. They are decorated with red and blue glass.

Iron Age warriors

The Romans believed that the tribes of Iron Age Britain were constantly fighting one another. Certainly, from time to time, warriors from rival tribes would invade and capture each other's territory, plunder their hillforts, and then burn the buildings to the ground.

Weapons of war

Iron Age warriors included women as well as men. They carried various weapons adapted for different uses:

a long sword for slashing at the enemy...

...a wooden shield for protection...

...and an iron-tipped spear for throwing.

Fierce fighters

Iron Age warriors fought on foot and on swift war chariots pulled by horses. A chariot carried two people – a driver and a soldier. They would rush into a battle on their chariot. The soldier would jump off to fight, and then leap back onto it to move on.

According to Roman writers, Celtic warriors often went into battle naked, apart from sword belts, bands around their arms, and torcs around their necks. Sometimes they painted their bodies with blue dye to make themselves look even more intimidating.

Into battle

A typical battle would begin with an individual warrior challenging a particular enemy fighter to a duel. Sometimes these one-to-one battles would put an end to a dispute between rival tribes.

Fighters from both tribes would watch the duel. If there was no clear winner, they would charge at each other roaring at the tops of their voices or singing loud battle songs as they attacked.

The resulting frenzy could be effective against enemies who weren't used to it. But if they were defeated, many warriors would kill themselves rather than be captured – prisoners were often used as slaves.

The art of war

Although Iron Age Britons may not have loved war quite as much as
the Romans thought, some of the finest examples of Celtic art and
craftsmanship found in Britain have been military
equipment. This is a sign that warriors were very
important in Iron Age society.

The warrior who wore this
torc must have had a very
strong neck. It's solid gold,
and weighs 1kg (about 2lbs).

This iron
sword,
decorated with
bronze and red
glass, was
buried with its
owner at
Kirkburn in
Lancashire.

This ornate shield
was probably used
for show rather
than in battle, as
it was too short
and thin to
protect anyone.

Fighting the Romans

By the 1st century BC, the Romans had spread out
from the city of Rome to conquer much of Europe. The
Roman general Julius Caesar conquered Gaul (Iron
Age France), and in 55BC, he invaded Britain, too.

Caesar and his troops landed on the south coast, but
they were driven off by local warriors. He returned
the following year with a bigger army.
This time, he won many victories, but
he still wasn't able to stay long enough
to conquer the island.

The invading Romans
didn't use chariots in
battle. They were
fascinated by British
battle chariots. Rich
Romans even asked
soldiers to bring
them back as
souvenirs.

Meet the people

Although few skeletons from the Iron Age have been found, the remains of men and women have been uncovered in the peat bogs of Britain and other parts of Europe.

While bones may dissolve or crumble to dust, chemicals in peat can preserve the skin, clothing and even the hair and internal organs of bodies buried there. Sometimes even the contents of their stomachs have been preserved. All this material can be used to create clear images of some of the people who lived in Iron Age Britain.

Using the preserved remains of a body found in a peat bog near Lindow Moss, experts were able to reconstruct the face of an Iron Age man.

Lindow Man

In 1984, the top half of a man's body was discovered by workmen cutting peat at Lindow Moss in Cheshire. From the preserved remains, scientists have been able to determine all sorts of things about him.

Lindow Man, as he is now known, was a healthy man in his mid-20s who died around 2,000 years ago. Standing about 1.73m (5ft 8in) tall, he had dark brown hair, and a neatly trimmed beard and moustache. His fingernails were well manicured, so he was probably not a hard worker, and may have been quite wealthy.

Lindow Man met a gruesome end. He was strangled, knocked on the head and his throat was cut It's not clear which of these actually killed him. Then his dead body was pushed face down into the peat.

Some experts think that this elaborate killing was part of a ceremonial sacrifice. Lindow Man may even have volunteered to die in this way, believing it to be a sacred duty. Others think he was a criminal who was executed as punishment.

Lindow Man had a last meal of bread, wheat and barley cooked over a fire of heather twigs.

Clonycavan man

The top half of another man was discovered in 2003 in Clonycavan in Ireland. A little shorter than Lindow Man, he stood about 1.57m (5ft 2in) tall. He had met a similarly violent end, perhaps as another victim of a ritual sacrifice, but around 300 years earlier.

Study of his hair has revealed that his recent diet was rich in vegetables, which could narrow the time of his death to the summer months.

This incredibly well-preserved hand comes from a man who lived some time between 362BC and 175BC. His body was found in a peat bog at Oldcroghan in Ireland.

The height of fashion

One of the most amazing things about Clonycavan Man's hair, however, is that he was using a type of styling gel to make it stick up — most likely the fashionable way for men to wear their hair at the time. The gel was made from plant oil and pine resin imported from France or Spain, and would have been very expensive. Like Lindow Man, it seems Clonycavan Man was a wealthy individual.

Over the centuries, chemicals in the peat have stained Clonycavan Man's hair and skin ginger brown.

Cast in bronze

Images of Iron Age Britons are very rare, but this small bronze head is 2,000 years old. It was found at a late Iron Age burial in Hertfordshire, and it shows a man with his hair combed back and a large well-groomed moustache.

Mythology and history

Although we have the remains of only a few Iron Age people, others are known to us through myths that have been passed down through the generations.

Every tribe in Iron Age Britain had its own poet, or bard, whose job it was to memorize and recite classic tales about the past, and to make up new ones about his tribe's most famous victories.

Legends of the land

Celtic myths, including the Irish 'Fenian Cycle' and the Welsh 'Mabinogion', are filled with larger-than-life heroes, doomed romances, foul treachery, bloody battles and magical animals. These dramatic tales often attempt to explain the origins of the people and the land where they lived.

One story tells how the hero of the Fenian Cycle, a giant named Fionn mac Cumhaill, or Finn McCool, built a rock formation known as Giant's Causeway, so he could cross the sea from Ireland to Scotland to fight a rival giant there.

This is Giant's Causeway, in Northern Ireland.

Legend says it was built by a giant named Finn McCool, but in fact it was formed from cooling lava after a volcano erupted over 50 million years ago.

Iron Age Britons didn't know how to read and write, so these tales were passed on by word of mouth and weren't written down for centuries.

The stories probably changed a lot in between, but they may still contain some grains of truth about the lives of great Iron Age heroes.

The reality of Rome

Unlike prehistoric bog bodies and characters from Celtic myths, some Iron Age Britons are part of written history. Romans were in regular contact with Britain from around 100BC, and they wrote down lots of details about the people they met. Caesar himself wrote an account of his invasions, and even recorded the names of some of the chiefs who fought against him, including Cassivelaunus, who also appears in the Mabinogion.

In the year 43, the Romans invaded Britain again. Within a few years, it was clear they were going to stay for a long, long time. A new age was already underway for the people of Britain.

The Children of Lir

An Irish legend tells the misfortunes of a man called Lir. He had four children with his first wife, but his second wife was jealous of them. She cursed them all to become swans, and bound them with silver chains.

A kindly monk broke the curse 900 years later, only to watch them turn back into people and die of old age.

Timeline of Prehistoric Britain

Ever since planet Earth was formed, the land that would become the British Isles has undergone many changes, and has been home to all sorts of creatures.

Around 4.5 thousand million years ago: planet Earth is formed.

Around 3.7 thousand million years ago: blue-green algae, the earliest living thing, appears.

Around 500 million years ago: volcanoes erupt across Britain. Mountains including Scafell Pike are formed.

PRECAMBRIAN SUPER-EON: up until 550 million years ago

PALAEOZOIC ERA: 550-250 million years ago

Ammonites

Britain

Pangaea

Around 250 million years ago: there is only one continent, known as Pangaea. The land that would become Britain is roughly in the middle of it.

About 350-250 million years ago: the Earth is in the grip of an ice age. Many living things die out.

TRIASSIC PERIOD: 250-200 million years ago

Dimetrodon – an ancestor of the dinosaurs

Lungfish

Spiny shark

The first dinosaurs appear in the Triassic period.

Dimorphodon – a flying reptile

Diplodocus

JURASSIC PERIOD: 200-145 million years ago

Jurassic Britain is much warmer than today. Dinosaurs thrive in this climate.

Cretaceous Britain is mostly under water. It's home to giant swimming reptiles.

65 million years ago: a meteor crashes into Earth, leading to the death of the dinosaurs.

55 million years ago: mammals have spread all over the Earth.

CRETACEOUS PERIOD: 145-65 million years ago

PALAEOGENE PERIOD: 65-23 million years ago

Ichthyosaurus

Moeritherium

About 20 million years ago: a new ice age begins.

30 million years ago: Britain has moved north, roughly where it is today. But it's attached to the mainland.

NEOGENE PERIOD: 23-2.6 million years ago

Britain

About 4 million years ago: the first human-like creatures appear in Africa.

Europe

About 2 million years ago: the Earth enters another ice age.

During the coldest cycles of this ice age, much of Britain is buried under thick ice. Most plants and animals can't survive there.

PLEISTOCENE EPOCH: 2.6-0.5 million years ago

About 500,000 years ago: Britain enters a warm period. People hunt elephants there.

People in Britain make lots of handaxes.

The oldest traces of human life in Britain date back to 750,000 years ago.

LOWER PALAEOLITHIC AGE: 2.5 million-100,000 years ago

About 400,000 years ago: another glaciation period sets in. It's too cold for people or animals to live in Britain.

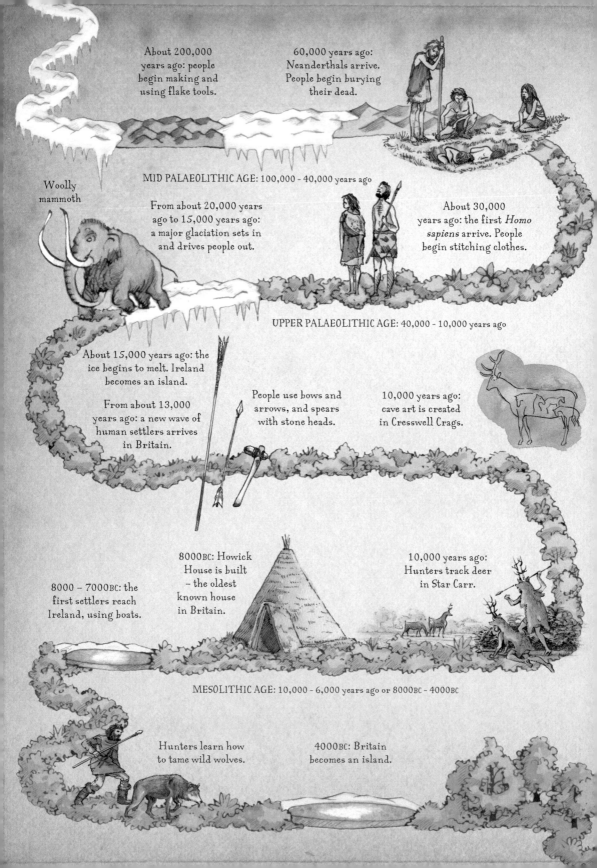

About 200,000 years ago: people begin making and using flake tools.

60,000 years ago: Neanderthals arrive. People begin burying their dead.

MID PALAEOLITHIC AGE: 100,000 - 40,000 years ago

Woolly mammoth

From about 20,000 years ago to 15,000 years ago: a major glaciation sets in and drives people out.

About 30,000 years ago: the first *Homo sapiens* arrive. People begin stitching clothes.

UPPER PALAEOLITHIC AGE: 40,000 - 10,000 years ago

About 15,000 years ago: the ice begins to melt. Ireland becomes an island.

From about 13,000 years ago: a new wave of human settlers arrives in Britain.

People use bows and arrows, and spears with stone heads.

10,000 years ago: cave art is created in Cresswell Crags.

8000BC: Howick House is built – the oldest known house in Britain.

10,000 years ago: Hunters track deer in Star Carr.

8000 – 7000BC: the first settlers reach Ireland, using boats.

MESOLITHIC AGE: 10,000 - 6,000 years ago or 8000BC - 4000BC

Hunters learn how to tame wild wolves.

4000BC: Britain becomes an island.

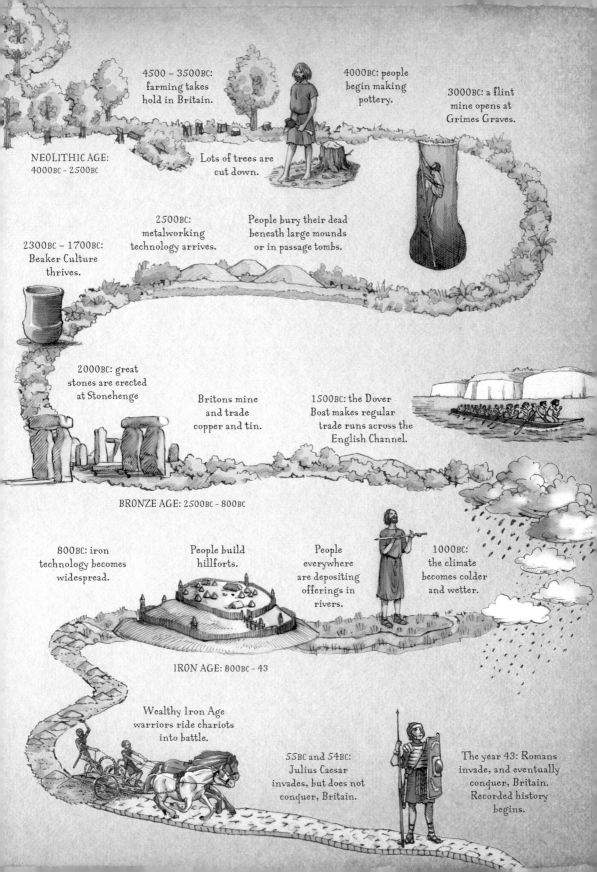

4500 – 3500BC: farming takes hold in Britain.

4000BC: people begin making pottery.

3000BC: a flint mine opens at Grimes Graves.

NEOLITHIC AGE: 4000BC – 2500BC

Lots of trees are cut down.

2500BC: metalworking technology arrives.

People bury their dead beneath large mounds or in passage tombs.

2300BC – 1700BC: Beaker Culture thrives.

2000BC: great stones are erected at Stonehenge

Britons mine and trade copper and tin.

1500BC: the Dover Boat makes regular trade runs across the English Channel.

BRONZE AGE: 2500BC – 800BC

800BC: iron technology becomes widespread.

People build hillforts.

People everywhere are depositing offerings in rivers.

1000BC: the climate becomes colder and wetter.

IRON AGE: 800BC – 43

Wealthy Iron Age warriors ride chariots into battle.

55BC and 54BC: Julius Caesar invades, but does not conquer, Britain.

The year 43: Romans invade, and eventually conquer, Britain. Recorded history begins.

Prehistoric Britain today

This map shows where some of the most interesting
remains from prehistoric Britain were found.
Many are open for visitors to see.

Key:

- Pre-human
- Paleolithic
- Mesolithic
- Neolithic
- Bronze Age
- Iron Age

Ring of Brodgar
standing stones

Skara Brae settlement

Maeshowe
passage tomb

Callanish stones
monument

Càrn Liath
broch

Eilean Dòmhnuill
crannog

Lealt shale
dinosaur fossils

Clava Cairn
tomb

Cladh Hallan
mummies

Mither Tap
hillfort

Coll Island crannogs
and brochs

Kilmartin Glen
standing stones

Loch Lomond

Edin's Hall broch

Dumbarton
Castle

Cramond
hunting camp

Howick House

Giant's
Causeway

Grianan of
Aileach stone fort

Torhouse
standing stones

Mayburgh
henge

Céide Fields
farmland

Carrowmore
passage tomb

Castlerigg
stone circle

Scafell Pike

Thornborough
henges

Star Carr settlement

Corlea
Trackway

Newgrange
passage tomb

Wetwang
chariot burials

Clonycavan
Man

Great
Orme copper
mine

Ferriby
boats

Dún Aonghasa
stone fort

Oldcroghan Man

Bryn Celli Ddu
passage tomb

Mold
cape

Lindow
Man

Creswell Crags
cave art

Seahenge monument

Craggaunowen
crannogs

Tre'r Cieri
hillfort

Capel Garmon

Flag Fen
settlement

Snettisham
treasures

Dunmore
Caves

Carrigagulla
stone circle

Pen Dinas
hillfort

Mitchell's Fold
stone circle

Grimes
Graves
flint mine

Clegyr Boia
settlement

Paviland Cave
skeleton

Uffington Horse

Mount Gabriel
copper mine

Gough's Cave
Cheddar Man

Devil's
Dyke ditch

The Sweet
Track

Avebury and
Silbury Hill

Julliberrie's Grave
long barrow

Hembury
causewayed
enclosure

Jurassic
Coast
dinosaur
fossils

Maiden Castle

Stonehenge

Boxgrove
handaxes

Dover Boat

Compton Bay
dinosaur footprints

Lanyon Quoit
dolmen monument

Glossary

This glossary explains some of the words used in this book. If a word is written in *italic* type, it has an entry of its own.

archaeology The study of humankind, by examining remains and artefacts which are often found underground.

barrow A large mound of earth, often built to mark a place where people are buried.

Beaker Culture A way of life common in western Europe during the Early Bronze Age, notable for its drinking pots.

Bronze Age A period of time during which metalwork was introduced. In Britain, it lasted from about 2500BC-800BC.

cannibals People who eat other people, either for food or as part of a *ritual*.

Celts A collection of groups of people who lived in Europe over 2,000 years ago.

clans Communities that are all part of the same *tribe*.

climate The average weather conditions for an area, usually based on temperature and rainfall.

cremation Burning a body after a person has died.

Druid The Roman name for a Celtic priest.

flint knapping The art of creating tools by chipping rocks, especially flint.

glaciation A period of extreme cold weather, when *glaciers* cover much of the Earth.

glaciers Huge sheets of ice.

handaxe One of the oldest stone tools, used by early types of human beings.

henges Sacred monuments built in a circle, often marked by standing stones.

hillforts Places built on top of hills, used as *settlements* and defensive spaces.

history An account of events of the past, since the development of writing.

hunter-gatherers People who live by hunting, fishing and collecting wild fruits and nuts.

ice ages Periods of time in which the *climate* is cold enough that *glaciers* cover the north and south poles.

Iron Age A period of time in which many tools were made from iron. In Britain, it began in about 800BC and ended with the arrival of the Romans. In Ireland it ended in around the year 400.

Mesolithic Age Middle Stone Age – a period of time in which people were mostly *hunter-gatherers*, but made sophisticated tools and artefacts. In Britain, it lasted from about 8000BC-4500BC.

myths Ancient stories that often attempt to explain the origins of a group of people and the land where they live, including exaggerated versions of real people as well as supernatural beings.

Neanderthal A type of early human, who lived in Europe from about 200,000-30,000 years ago.

Neolithic Age New Stone Age – a period of time during which farming, pottery and house-building took off. In Britain, it ran from about 4500BC-2500BC.

Palaeolithic Age Old Stone Age – a period of time in which people began to make simple tools made of stone, bone and wood. In Britain, it lasted from about 800,000-10,000 years ago.

passage tomb An underground burial chamber, built at the end of a passageway beneath a mound.

prehistory An account of the past from a time before the development of the written word.

ritual A ceremony, often performed as part of religious worship.

sacrifice Giving up an object of value, or killing an animal or person, often as an offering to a god.

settlement A group of dwellings, that form a community.

smelting Heating up rocks to extract metals contained within them.

tribe A group of people, usually one that has not developed a written language, that shares common ancestry, cultural, religious and regional origins.

Index

Acknowledgements

Every effort has been made to trace and acknowledge ownership of copyright. If any rights have been omitted, the publishers offer to rectify this in any future editions following notification. The publishers are grateful to the following individuals and organizations for their permission to reproduce material on the following pages: (t=top, b=bottom, l=left, r=right)

cover (t) © Adam Woolfitt/Corbis, **(b)** © Cultura RM/alamy;
p2-3 Ring of Brodgar, Orkney Islands ©Patrick Dieudonne/Getty Images; **p6** digital illustration of two diplodocuses by Peter Minister, background forest © Don Johnston/Alamy;
p7 Mike Agliolo/Science Photo Library; **p12** © The Natural History Museum, London;
p13 © The Natural History Museum, London; **p14** © The Trustees of the British Museum;
p15 Pascal Goetgheluck/Science Photo Library; **p16** photo © English Heritage/NMR; line drawing © Paul Brown; **p17** © The Natural History Museum, London; **p20** © Peter Howard;
p22 © The Trustees of the British Museum; **p23** © The Natural History Museum, London
p24 © Salisbury & South Wiltshire Museum; **p25** © David Lyons/Alamy; **p26-27** © Worldwide Picture Library / Alamy; **p27** © National Museums Scotland; **p29** all © The Trustees of the British Museum; **p30** IIC/ Axiom/Getty Images; **p31** © Bjanka Kadic/Alamy; **p32-33** © Adam Woolfitt/Corbis; **p34** © Wessex Archaeology 2007; **p35** both photos © The Trustees of the British Museum; **p37 (t)** © The Trustees of the British Museum, **(b)** Skyscan/Science Photo Library;
p38 © Ashmolean Museum, University of Oxford, UK/The Bridgeman Art Library;
p39 © John Henshall / Alamy; **p40-41** © James Beatty, Courtesy of Flag Fen;
p42 © Amgueddfa Cymru - National Museum of Wales; **p43** © Skyscan/Corbis;
p44 © The Trustees of the British Museum; **p45** © The Trustees of the British Museum;
p46-47 © Norman Price/Alamy; **p49** © The Trustees of the British Museum; **p51** all © The Trustees of the British Museum; **p52** © The Trustees of the British Museum; **p53 (t)** © National Museum of Ireland, **(bl)** © National Museum of Ireland; **(br)** © The Trustees of the British Museum; **p54-55** © Tony Pleavin/Photolibrary

Additional illustrations by Peter Minister and Inklink Firenze
Additional editorial material by Megan Cullis
Additional designs by Brenda Cole, Anna Gould and Steve Wood
Digital design by John Russell

Picture research by Ruth King
with thanks to the British Museum